MW01503802

WORKBOOK

For

The 22 Immutable Laws Of

Branding

Diana Print

This workbook belongs to

_____

_____

_____

©COPYRIGHT 2023 -ALL RIGHTS RESERVED

All copyrights are retained. No portion of this workbook may be mechanically, electronically, or otherwise copied or communicated, including by photocopying.

Disclaimer

Unofficially, this workbook serves as the original book's companion. It has been written with the goal of summarizing the important ideas and concepts covered in the book to help readers understand the author's main point. The workbook also includes tasks and exercises to help readers comprehend and apply the author's main ideas to their own lives or routines.

How to use this workbook

The purpose of this workbook is to make it easier for you to understand and apply the major ideas from the main book to your particular situation. It is meant to improve your comprehension and absorption of the ideas rather than to replace the primary book. Please follow these rules to get the most out of this workbook:

1. Read the chapter in the main book that corresponds to each segment before beginning it. This will guarantee that you understand the key concepts and ideas that will be covered.

2. Finish the exercises and tasks included in each segment, which may include questions for reflection, writing assignments, and examples from real-world situations. This will increase your comprehension of and capacity for using the ideas from the main text.

3. Keep your life experiences in mind as you move through the workbook. This will help you make connections between the knowledge and your personal experiences, which will increase the possibility that you will implement the ideas.

4. Review and reevaluate your answers to the exercises and tasks after you've finished each section. This will improve your comprehension of the subject and serve as a reminder and future reference.

5. Go at your own pace and take your time. Immerse yourself in the material because this workbook is meant to be a personal journey of learning and growth. While some exercises can be finished in a single sitting, others might call for more thought and reflection.

This workbook's goal is to aid in your comprehension and practical application of the main book's major concepts. You can make positive changes in your daily life by actively participating in the exercises and thinking back on your own experience. This workbook acts as a manual for understanding the important concepts discussed in the main book.

Write your affirmations for the book

Summary of the main book

The underlying ideas and tactics that underpin successful branding are examined in the book. It highlights the significance of creating a great brand and provides helpful advice on how to create and maintain a strong brand identity. According to the writers, branding is more about establishing a distinctive position in the market that appeals to consumers than it is about advertising or logo design.

22 unchangeable laws of branding are presented by the writers as a roadmap for brand managers and executives. The laws include everything from the value of

focusing more narrowly to the necessity of ongoing innovation and adaptability. The book uses numerous real-world examples of successful and unsuccessful branding campaigns to illustrate these principles.

The 22 laws of branding, as presented in the book, can be divided into four main groups based on their related themes:

Group 1: Creating a Strong Brand Foundation

The law of :

1. Expansion
2. Contraction
3. Publicity
4. Diversion
5. Attributes
6. Quality
7. Credentials
8. Extensions

Group 2: Building Brand Positioning

The law of :

9. the Name

10. the Generic

11. Singularity

12. Consumers

13. Fellowship

Group 3: Establishing Brand Consistency

The law of :

14. Advertising

15. Mortality

16. Line Extension

17. Sub Brands

18. Shape

19. Color

20. Borders

Group 4: Sustaining Brand Growth

The law of :

21. Consistency

22. Change

These groupings reflect the different aspects and stages of branding, from laying a strong foundation and positioning the brand in the market to maintaining consistency

Summary of Group one

Laying a Firm Foundation for Your Brand

This group's objective is building a strong brand foundation.

1. Expansion: According to this law, businesses shouldn't diversify into markets with unrelated goods or services. To develop a strong and unique brand identity, they should instead concentrate on and specialize in their core offering.

2. Contraction: In contrast to Expansion, this law suggests that companies concentrate on a small segment of the market. By focusing on a

particular topic, businesses may position themselves as authorities, stand out from rivals, and attract a certain target market.

3. Publicity: To increase their visibility and reputation, brands must generate publicity and high buzz. This law underlines how crucial it is to use public relations to increase brand recognition and perception as well as to generate favorable media coverage.

4. Diversion: Brands should refrain from focusing their attention and resources on pointless endeavors or activities that do not complement their core identity. Confusion and diminished brand

attractiveness can result from diverting attention or watering down the brand's core.

5. Attributes: A brand should be associated with particular qualities that appeal to its target market. Companies can successfully communicate their distinctive value offer and develop a distinct market position by highlighting key brand traits.

6. Quality: Businesses must give consistent high-quality performance to their goods and services as a top priority. Building trust, reputation, and consumer loyalty all depend heavily on quality. The

perceived value of the products has a significant impact on brand perception and reputation.

7. Credentials: Credentials such as expertise, qualifications, honors, or endorsements should be used by brands to generate credibility. Brands may build credibility and trust by exhibiting their credentials, which strengthens their position as dependable and trustworthy.

8. Extensions: This rule gives businesses advice on how to strategically increase the range of goods and services they offer. It underlines how crucial it is to expand the brand into related or

complimentary product categories that complement its key attributes and target market. Effective brand extensions use the current brand equity to expand into new areas or target new client categories.

The first collection of laws underlines the value of building a solid brand foundation. They help brands develop a distinctive identity that stands out in the marketplace, concentrate on their key capabilities, and make strategic decisions. Brands can position themselves for long-term success and growth by comprehending and putting these ideas into practice.

Key points

1. To develop a powerful and unique brand identity, concentrate on and specialize in your core offering.

2. To set yourself apart from rivals, focus on and target a particular market or niche.

3. Create favorable publicity and use PR to boost a brand's reputation and visibility.

4. Refrain from allocating funds to irrelevant or business operations that weaken the identity of your brand.

5. Identify and link your brand to particular qualities that appeal to your target market.

6. Give quality a high priority and uphold it throughout all of your goods and services.

7. Obtain credentials, such as expertise, qualifications, or endorsements, to establish credibility.

8. Strategically add similar or complimentary categories to your product or service offerings.

9. To foster consumer loyalty and trust, cultivate a solid reputation for dependability.

10. Establish a distinctive brand position that sets you apart from rivals and appeals to your target market.

Journal prompts

How can you concentrate your brand's efforts on a certain market or niche?

_____

_____

_____

_____

Consider a time when your brand earned favorable press. What effect did it have on brand recognition and reputation?

_____

_____

_____

_____

Are there any endeavors or projects that take away from the essence of your brand? How can you realign your efforts and refocus?

_____

_____

_____

_____

What qualities are relevant to your target audience? How can you highlight these qualities in your branding initiatives?

_____

_____

_____

_____

How can you continually provide high-quality goods or services to your clients to earn their confidence and loyalty?

_____

_____

_____

_____

What credentials can you emphasize to develop credibility and build the reputation of your brand?

_____

_____

_____

_____

How can you establish a solid reputation for your brand as being dependable and trustworthy?

_____

_____

_____

_____

Summary of group two

Brand Positioning Development

This group focuses on the vital process of creating a powerful brand positioning. These regulations dive into a variety of factors that establish and influence a brand's positioning in the marketplace. The following is an explanation of each law in this collection:

9. the Name: A brand's name has a big impact on how it is positioned. A strong brand identity can be developed with the aid of a well-chosen, memorable, and distinctive name.

10. the Generic: Companies that employ generic words frequently find it difficult to stand out from the competition. Avoiding generic names and phrases helps brands present themselves as distinctive and one-of-a-kind.

11. Singularity: To differentiate themselves from rivals, brands must develop a distinctive selling proposition. Building a distinct and appealing brand positioning requires being distinctive and providing something unusual.

12. Consumers: For successful brand positioning, it is essential to comprehend the target market. Brands may position

themselves to satisfy those particular consumer expectations by carefully studying their wants, preferences, and desires.

13. Fellowship: Brands might gain from teaming up with complementary goods or services that appeal to the same target market. This link can improve brand positioning and foster deep relationships with consumers.

Brands can create a compelling and distinctive brand positioning by adhering to these laws. A memorable and distinctive name must be carefully chosen, generic terminology must be avoided, unique selling points must be highlighted, the target audience must be completely understood, and strategic brand alliances must be taken into account.

Brands may stand out in the crowded market and draw in their ideal customers by developing a strong brand positioning. It enables them to successfully express their value proposition and develop a foundation of devoted customers.

Key points

1. A successful brand identity must start with a carefully considered and memorable brand name.

2. When branding yourself, stay away from general terminology to set yourself apart from rivals.

3. Discover a USP that differentiates your brand and appeals to your target market.

4. Effective brand positioning requires an understanding of your target audience's needs, interests, and desires.

5. Create strategic alliances with businesses that share your values to improve the positioning of your brand.

6. Clearly outline and successfully express your brand's value proposition.

7. Carry out market research to find market gaps and chances for differentiation.

8. Tailor your brand messaging to appeal to the intellect and emotions of your target market.

9. Constantly assess and modify your brand positioning in light of customer and market trends.

10. To develop authenticity and foster trust, match your brand positioning with your brand's guiding principles.

Journal prompts

Consider how the name of your company now affects your positioning. Does it support the identity of your brand?

_____

_____

_____

_____

Come up with alternate, recognizable names or terms for your brand to use in the marketplace.

_____

_____

_____

_____

Determine what makes you special. What distinguishes your company's brand from rivals?

———————————————————
———————————————————
———————————————————
———————————————————

Clearly describe who your target market is. How can you position your brand to fulfill their particular needs?

———————————————————
———————————————————
———————————————————
———————————————————

Look into possible strategic alliances with companies whose target market is comparable to yours.

_____

_____

_____

_____

Assess the value proposition and messaging of your present brand. How can it be improved?

_____

_____

_____

_____

Conduct market research to find areas where your industry is lacking and chances to stand out.

_____

_____

_____

_____

Summary of group three

Establishing Brand Consistency

This body of laws emphasizes how crucial it is to keep all branding components consistent to build a powerful and recognizable brand identity.

14. Advertising: Consumers are more likely to associate a brand with its message and image when there is consistency in its advertising. Advertisements should retain a consistent tone and visual style and be in line with the overall company positioning.

15.   Mortality: For brands to remain relevant, they must change and adapt. Neglecting shifts in consumer tastes or market dynamics may cause a brand to deteriorate and ultimately fail.

16.   Line Extension: A brand's identity can be diluted and consumers may become confused if it extends into too many product categories. It's crucial to carefully analyze brand extensions and make sure they complement the spirit of the main brand.

17.   Subbrands: Subbrands should maintain their unique identities while being consistent with the parent brand.

Although subbrands might serve certain target markets or product categories, they should support and reinforce the overall brand image.

18. Shape: A brand's product or logo's physical shape or design can help with recognition and distinctiveness. Consistency in shapes enables customers to recognize and connect particular shapes with a specific brand.

19. Color: Using color consistently can help build strong brand recognition. Establishing a visual identity that clients can relate to the company is made easier by choosing specific colors and utilizing

them consistently throughout branding materials.

20. Borders: Delineating the brand's positioning and services inside those limitations helps to maintain consistency and avoid brand dilution. Building a defined brand image and outlining the brand's inclusions and exclusions aid in perception shaping.

Key points

1. To reinforce the brand message and image, advertising must be consistent.

2. The long-term success of the brand depends on the brand evolving and adapting to shifting consumer tastes and market conditions.

3. To avoid dilution and preserve brand integrity, carefully examine brand extensions.

4. While remaining aligned with the parent brand, subbrands should have their own unique identities.

5. The physical form or design components can aid in brand uniqueness and awareness.

6. Maintaining color constancy is important for creating a distinguishable brand identity.

7. Clearly defining the brand's positioning boundaries helps to maintain consistency and avoid brand dilution.

Journal prompts

Picture a business that makes effective use of consistent advertising. What elements contribute to the coherence of their messaging?

_____

_____

_____

_____

Consider examples of brands that were unable to adapt to changing market conditions. What is to be concluded from their mistakes?

_____

_____

_____

Study a business that has used subbrands successfully. In the overall brand strategy, what part do these subbrands play?

_____

_____

_____

_____

Take into account how shape impacts brand recognition. Mention businesses whose recognizable icons once served as their logos.

_____

_____

_____

_____

Think about the branding strategies used by companies in various industries. How do these strategies follow the guidelines for design, color, and advertising consistency?

_____

_____

_____

_____

Discuss the impact of brand consistency on customer perception and loyalty. How does a consistent brand experience affect brand loyalty and customer trust?

_____

_____

_____

_____

Summary of group four

Brand Growth Sustainment

This team focuses on the ongoing activities required to sustain brand growth and adapt to the marketplace.

21. Consistency: To encourage customer loyalty and trust, consistency in branding elements such as language, imagery, and customer experience must be established and preserved.

22. Change: Brands must continuously evolve and adapt to meet the changing needs and preferences of consumers. Stasis or unwillingness to change can make a brand irrelevant.

Key points

1. Consistently deliver on your brand promise to earn clients' trust and confidence.

2. Embrace change and be open to adjusting your brand techniques if you want to stay relevant in a market that is changing.

3. Monitor consumer trends and preferences constantly to identify opportunities for brand expansion.

4. Continue to engage in market research and consumer feedback to understand changing consumer expectations and wants.

5. Be proactive in identifying potential hazards or hurdles to your brand's

growth and create plans to cope with them.

6. To maintain a competitive advantage, seek for opportunities for innovation and originality.

7. Encourage an agile and adaptive corporate culture to help your business effectively respond to market developments.

8. To take into account shifting consumer beliefs and behaviors, regularly review and modify your brand positioning and message.

9. Keep an eye out for emerging platforms and technologies that can be used to boost brand awareness and engagement.

10. Develop positive relationships with key stakeholders, including customers, employees, and influential members of the industry, to enhance the reputation of your brand and support its growth.

Journal prompts

Take into account the value of consistent branding. How have repeated brand experiences impacted your opinion of a specific company or product?

_____

_____

_____

_____

Provide an instance of a brand that successfully adapted to market developments. What strategies did they employ, and how did that influence their growth?

_____

_____

_____

Identify a brand that has been effective in utilizing new platforms or technologies. How did this impact their growth and degree of customer engagement?

Take into account your brand or a different well-known brand. Exist any potential challenges or threats the brand might face in the future? How can they stop them in their tracks?

Take into account how market research and consumer input can help a brand continue to grow. How can companies use these insights to change the requirements of their customers?

_____

_____

_____

_____

All success comes from consistency.

Notes

Notes

_____

_____

_____

_____

_____

_____

_____

_____

_____

Notes

Notes

Notes

_____

_____

_____

_____

_____

_____

_____

_____

Made in the USA
Las Vegas, NV
29 November 2023

81794475R00036